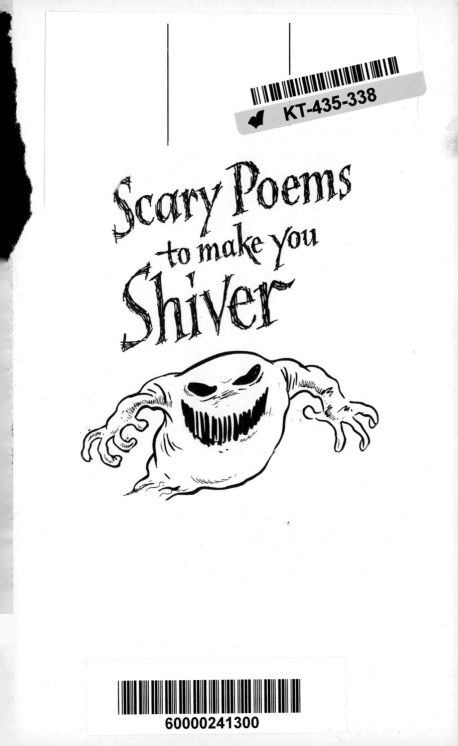

Scary Poems to make you Shiver

Look out for other books by Susie Gibbs:

Funny Poems to Give You the Giggles
Revolting Poems to Make You Squirm
Puzzling Poems to Drive You Crazy

Scary Poems to make you Shiver

Collected by Susie Gibbs

Illustrated by Martin Chatterton

OXFORD
UNIVERSITY PRESS

OXFORD

UNIVERSITY PRESS

Great Clarendon Street, Oxford OX2 6DP

Oxford University Press is a department of the University of Oxford.
It furthers the University's objective of excellence in research, scholarship,
and education by publishing worldwide in

Oxford   New York

Auckland   Cape Town   Dar es Salaam   Hong Kong   Karachi
Kuala Lumpur   Madrid   Melbourne   Mexico City   Nairobi
New Delhi   Shanghai   Taipei   Toronto

With offices in

Argentina   Austria   Brazil   Chile   Czech Republic   France   Greece
Guatemala   Hungary   Italy   Japan   Poland   Portugal   Singapore
South Korea   Switzerland   Thailand   Turkey   Ukraine   Vietnam

Oxford is a registered trade mark of Oxford University Press
in the UK and in certain other countries

This selection and arrangement © Susie Gibbs 2006
Illustrations copyright © Martin Chatterton 2006

ISBN-13: 978-0-19-272607-0

5 7 9 10 8 6 4

Printed in Great Britain

Paper used in the production of this book is a natural, recyclable
product made from wood grown in sustainable forests. The manufacturing
process conforms to the environmental regulations of the country of origin.

Contents

The Cupboard Under the Sink

In the dark, dripping depths
of the cupboard under the sink,
school spiders stalk.
Their eyes glint and stare.
Cricked, thick legs stick
through cracks in the door.
They don't spin webs. No.
Flies are too small and
wings flicker and tickle
in the back of their throats.
They want children,
to wrap in their strong bristled limbs,
to pull onto the piles of painting palettes,
to feed on in the darkness.
Yes, the spiders are hungry
and they want children.
They want children.

THEY WANT YOU!

Mark Halliday

Don't Panic

That beating at my bedroom pane:
It's only wind and driving rain.
Relax.

That monstrous shadow leaning in,
Wearing an evil twisted grin:
It's just the ivy plant, that's all,
Bobbing and tossing on the wall.
Don't panic.

That rustling: is it just the draught?
Or giant spiders? Don't be daft!
Couldn't be.

The loops this new wallpaper makes:
Just loops, not coiled and deadly snakes.
Keep cool.

Suppose there are though—snakes, I mean,
And evil spirits sliding in,
And ghosts and blobs and phantom riders
And armies of advancing spiders,
And vampires stalking through the gloom,
All closing in upon my room . . .

HELP!

Eric Finney

Watching

What if I told you
The stars in the sky
Were not really stars at all

But eyes

Winking blinking
And spying on you
Watching your every move

Try and imagine it

Now try to fall asleep
On a clear night
If you can.

Andrea Shavick

When the Moon Went Mad . . .

Something scrapes on my door
There's blood on the floor
A tall shadow shivers
And gives me the quivers
I pull my nose under my duvet tonight
I turn to the wall and shut my eyes tight
The moon swims up to my window and grins
When I turn back to look, it gatecrashes in
Its horrible grin has turned to a howl
Wolves in the street are out on the prowl
My door is torn open, a wind chills my spine
Seaweeds are floating, the blood looks like wine
In the greenish moonshine
The wolves dance and whine
The seaweeds spin round
As I feel myself drown
Unable to scream
And wake from this dream.

Bashabi Fraser

A Better Mousetrap

If you build a better mousetrap
And put it in your house,
Before long, Mother Nature's
Going to build a better mouse.

Anon.

Roses Are Red

Roses are red,
Spiders are black,
Don't look now
But there's one on your back!

Anon.

A Night I Had Trouble Falling Asleep

I stayed over at Eliot's house.
'I've lost my pet,' he said.
'So please wake me up in the middle of the night
If you find a big snake in your bed.'

Jeff Moss

A Fear

I waited for you all the time,
   but you never came.
I don't think you ever had such
   a firm shape before.
Or perhaps it was just that I
   only realized it that day under the bed,
waiting for you to crawl out,
   and remembering your pipe-cleaner legs
in the poem Merle Kobatake
   wrote about you
in the toe of her shoe.

I watched on the concrete pavement
   outside my flat in Waikiki.
I listened to the story of how
   you once crouched
on a man's back, in a kimono,
   up the valley in Manoa.
But you never came.
   I remember the book
with your picture in it
   the boys had in Kaneohe,
a bit dog-eared, and as if borrowed.

But it was you all right,
    there as in the film
when Sean Connery woke up
    naked from his bath with
you on his shoulder.
    It must be the shoulder
for me that the vulnerable place
    is in, where I feel
the prickly, gooseflesh horror
    and turn, anguished, striking,
finding you even bigger than I expected.

George MacBeth

Someone at the Door
(a poem for two voices)

Knock, knock.
'Who's there?'
'A traveller.'
'What do you want?'
'Somewhere to stay.'
'Are you mad!
This is no hotel.
Go away!'

Knock, knock.
'Who's there?'
'Me. It's still me.'
'The traveller?'
*'Yes. This is the place
I want to be.
Let me in.'*
'No!'

Knock, knock.
'Let me in!'
'A stranger?
At this time of night?
On your bike!
Get off,
or I'll set the dog on you!'
'I wouldn't, if I were you.'

Knock, knock.
'That's it!
Come on, Rex,
let's open this door.
Now will you . . .
Typical! Nobody there!'
'Oh, yes, there is.
And I'm in!'

Patricia Leighton

Whispers

Filled with the smell of damp and decay
The old mill slowly crumbles away,
But lingering still in the shadowy air
Are whispers of fear and cold despair
As ghost children, locked in a distant time,
Stare through windows cobwebbed with grime,
Their eyes frosty as starlight.

Cynthia Rider

Mr Alucard

Down our street there's someone new
Living next to the churchyard:
He is a man of mystery
Called Mr Alucard.
That's a strange name for starters,
But there's more that mystifies:
His wolfish grin, his sharp white teeth,
His very piercing eyes.
Wrapped in a big, black, batlike cloak
He goes out late at night
And I swear he casts no shadow
As he passes the street light.
Yesterday he said to me,
'What a lovely throat you've got.'
And he stared and smiled a secret smile;
It worries me a lot.
There's something odd about his name . . .
I can't think what it is,
And I'd like to make some sense
Of those weird ways of his.
I definitely need some help,
So please try very hard
To help me solve the mystery
Of Mr Alucard.

Eric Finney

The Phantom Footsteps

Footsteps ring out, loud and clear
but the walker knows there's no one there.
The alley's narrow, shadows fall
and slither down the dripping walls.
The walker hurries, runs. Behind,
the phantom steps unhinge his mind,
echoing, thundering, round his ears.
Sprinting now, he screams in fear,
then spins to face them, gasps for breath,
very nearly scared to death,
by an empty alley, silent, still.
He shivers with a sudden chill
and walks off briskly. Just behind,
shadows reach out, groping, blind.

Marian Swinger

The Void

Look into my face
And take a pace
Into a wilderness
Of driftwood, dunes, and sand.
A no man's land.

Step inside my head,
Inspect the empty bed,
The room swept bare,
No clue. No mess.
No forwarding address.

Tune into my mind,
Rewind
The silent spools and brush
The bat-winged echoes from your hair.
I am not there.

Sue Cowling

Just a Thought

I'm creeping up behind you,
inside you, I blind you,
I'm the darkness,
bad voices in your head.

I'm fear, ten feet tall,
the shadow on the wall,
I'm the coldness
that creeps in your bed.

I'm the horror in your mind,
I'm cruel and unkind,
I'm the devil
that wakes you at night.

You don't know who I am?
Good, that was my plan—
I'm just a *scary thought*
that gives you . . . a

FRIGHT!

Matt Black

The Ghostly Visitor

I wake up
In a pool of blue moonlight
The curtains are swaying
But there is no wind
The night is still and silent

Silent
Except for the clock
Ticking the minutes past midnight
And in the garden I hear
An eerie sound

An eerie sound
Like bones clicking
Or a body
Dragging itself over the autumn leaves
On the lawn
The sound of a rasping breath
Far away

Far away
But growing louder
Getting closer
The rustle of a branch against the wall
Or a claw
Scrabbling

Scrabbling
Beneath my window
Climbing
Trying to gain a purchase on the brick
I am frozen in my bed
Too scared to get up
And turn on the light
I lie still, listening
Until at last the sound recedes
Leaving my garden

Leaving my garden
But clearly heading
In the direction of
Your house

Your house . . .

Roger Stevens

Trick of the Lights

Late, late at night
you may never get home. They wink the word
from light to light

all down the long straight
empty road. Each one in turn will turn
against you, but they wait

green as grass on the opposite side
of a triptrap bridge, where amber teeth
and bloodshot eyes might hide

as you pedal for home, too fast. Too late.

Philip Gross

At Sunset

Men leave
The empty sepulchre,
Bewildered.

An owl hoots

As crosses,
Stakes,
And mallets
Are gladly
Packed away.

Laughter.

Relief.

But

In the undergrowth
A hand—skin like marble,
Nails like glass—
Pushes up
Through the soil

Fingers uncoiled
And flexing . . .

Kevin McCann

Toilet Monster

The invisible monster
who lives down the loo,
lies under the water
and waits for you.

It's no good deciding
to pull the chain,
to try and flush him
down the drain.

He clings to the bend
with teeth and claws,
with rolling eyes
and gnashing jaws.

And when you sit down
he's going to come
up out of the water
and bite your bum!

Geraldine Aldridge

Uncle John's Legs

It isn't the things that go bump in the night
It isn't the venom from Dracula's bite
It isn't the shadows that give me a fright
It's Uncle John's legs—all ghostly and white.

It isn't the howl of the wolf at the moon
It isn't the monster from in the lagoon
It isn't the sheen of green bones in the gloom
It's Uncle John's legs—they fill me with doom.

Unspeakably spindly, all ghoulish and glowing
Bubbling and bulgy blue blood vessels showing
Uncle John's legs keep to-ing and fro-ing
Following me wherever I'm going.

They infest my nightmares when I'm in my bed
Their echoing footsteps repeat in my head
But the strange thing is this . . . my Uncle John's dead
Yet I'm followed around by both of his legs
No body at all . . . just
                    both
                         of
                            his
                               legs . . .

Paul Cookson

Trick or Treat

We lurch along the darkened street
This spooky Hallowe'en
Freddy dressed as Frankenstein
His face a sickly green
Darren is dressed as a mummy
Bandaged from head to feet
Sarah is a scary ghost
Wrapped up in a sheet
I am dressed as Dracula
My cape is red and black
But I wish I knew who the zombie was
Creeping along at the back

Roger Stevens

Nightmare Questionnaire

Our chances of escape? *Zero*

When do you walk? *One a.m.*

Favourite hobbies? *Mayhem and Murder*

Favourite food? *Blood*

How do we stop you? *Impossible*

Where are you hiding? *Everywhere*

Favourite sound? *Screaming!*

Mike Johnson

Just the Usual Monsters

The house creaks, like it does in the wind.
Except that . . . tonight, there is no wind.
It could be a nightmare—it feels scary enough.
Except that . . . I'm not yet asleep.

There's a scuffling by the window,
The curtains ruffle, and here they are:
Horned, clawed, thick-set, scaly;
Blue, green, purple, blotchy.

Sickly grins, flared nostrils, yellow eyes;
Large as life, and twice as gruesome—
Though as they lumber across the floor towards me
They get strangely smaller, until, by the time they reach

My outstretched arm, each one is able, with a little effort,
To prise up my fingernails and slip underneath,
Ready to begin their mischievous journey
Below my skin.

After the initial agony, it feels more like
An unscratchable itch or a painful tickling.
I watch and feel their progress; the tiny bumps
Rippling upwards to my shoulder.

I know the routine—once in my neck
They start their fun, clambering up and down my arteries,
Playing about in my lungs, scampering around my
    intestines
And gingerly exploring my brain.

I've got used to them now—they're almost like friends.
When they leave, by the usual way, one or two
Even give a brief, backward wave, without looking.
The next morning, I tell my mother all about it.

'Just the usual monsters?' she asks, matter-of-factly;
I can tell she's other things on her mind.

Martin Brown

Demon Teddy

dearest Ted
with ribbon red
protect me from the nightly dread
of monsters underneath my bed

the light is off, goodnight's been said;
what are those horns upon your head?

Laura Sheridan

The Mistletoe Bough

The mistletoe hung in the castle hall,
The holly branch shone on the old oak wall;
And the baron's retainers were blithe and gay,
And keeping their Christmas holiday.
The baron beheld with a father's pride
His beautiful child, young Lovell's bride;
While she with her bright eyes seemed to be
The star of the goodly company.

'I'm weary of dancing now,' she cried;
'Here tarry a moment—I'll hide—I'll hide!
And, Lovell, be sure thou'rt the first to trace
The clue to my secret lurking place.'
Away she ran—and her friends began
Each tower to search and each nook to scan;
And young Lovell cried, 'Oh, where dost thou hide?
I'm lonesome without thee, my own dear bride.'
They sought her that night! and they sought her
    next day!
And they sought her in vain when a week passed away!
In the highest—the lowest—the loneliest spot,
Young Lovell sought wildly—but found her not.
And years flew by, and their grief at last
Was told as a sorrowful tale long past,
And when Lovell appeared, the children cried,
'See! the old man weeps for his fairy bride.'

At length an oak chest, that had long lain hid,
Was found in the castle—they raised the lid—
And a skeleton form lay mouldering there,
In the bridal wreath of that lady fair!
Oh! sad was her fate!—in sportive jest
She hid from her lord in the old oak chest.
It closed with a spring! and, dreadful doom,
The bride lay clasped in her living tomb!

Thomas Haynes Bayly

AARRGGH!!!!!!!

Making Friends

A new boy joined our class today.
His eyes are red, his skin is grey.
He will not come outside to play.
I think he needs a friend.

We set the goalposts on the grass.
We pick our teams, we strike and pass.
He's watching from behind the glass.
I'm sure he wants a friend.

A tackle causes injury.
Some blood is trickling from my knee.
I limp to class and there I see
The boy who has no friend.

He greets me with a sharp-toothed grin.
He licks his lips and helps me in.
Did I just hear him whispering?
Now you shall be my friend.

Rachel Rooney

The Party Guest

When Robert came to our house, late on Hallowe'en,
he was dressed as Dracula, best we'd ever seen.
He did a great impression, frightened all the guests,
he really seemed quite surprised we were so impressed.
He didn't say that much, but played our games all
  night,
in the apple bobbing he always got first bite.
Suddenly he was gone but we were all struck dumb
by knocking at the door and hearing Robert's mum,
'Sorry he didn't make it,' Robert's mother said.
'Robert's got the flu, you see, and he's at home in bed.'

Jane Saddler

The Fate of the Mary Belle

The Mary Belle was a pirate ship
Sailed by a murderous crew
And the day she was sunk you could hear the cheers
From Plymouth to Timbuktu.

The ship and the men sank together
Down to the soft seabed.
The timbers rotted and ravenous fish
Grew fat on loosened flesh.

Years passed by and the shifting sands,
Storms and the changing tides,
Rolled the remains of the Mary Belle
Shoreward and scattered them wide.

Holiday children searching for shells
Found knuckles of bone and teeth.
They threaded them into necklaces
To wear as they played on the beach.

The broken ship's wood fed barbecue fires
Which lit up the beach with their flames,
Threw sparks high up in the black night sky
And shone on the breaking waves.

With murderers' bones round their suntanned necks
The children danced and leapt,
Danced in the glowing firelight,
And shadows danced with them.

Patricia Leighton

Ghost-whispering

Skim an ice-chunk
Across a frozen pond's
Glittering skin until
It spins whispering

And if the ghosts come
Fog-drifting through twisted trees

Don't stand your ground
And don't look back

Just run . . .

Kevin McCann

Our Pond

The pond in our garden
Is murky and deep
And lots of things live there
That slither and creep,

Like diving bell spiders
And great rams-horn snails
And whirligig beetles
And black snappertails.

There used to be goldfish
That nibbled my thumb,
But now there's just algae
And sour, crusty scum.

There used to be pondweed
With fizzy green shoots,
But now there are leeches
And horrible newts.

One day when my football
Rolled in by mistake
I tried to retrieve it
By using a rake,

But as I leaned over
A shape from the ooze
Bulged up like a nightmare
And lunged at my shoes.

I ran back in shouting,
But everyone laughed
And said I was teasing
Or else I was daft.

But I know what happened
And when I'm asleep
I dream of those creatures
That slither and creep:

The diving bell spiders
And great rams-horn snails
And whirligig beetles
And black snappertails.

Richard Edwards

Munch Menu

Carrying a silver spoon and a glistening knife
And an enormous great pot;
Not keen on vegetables and fruit,
Nor apple pie piping hot;
In fact, he's hunting ingredients right now—
Boiling up water ready for the stew,
Adding a few herbs,
Licking his lips, looking at you!

Tim Pointon

Taking Care

There's a dungeon underneath our school
Where the caretaker keeps prisoners.
You hear them moaning when the wind
Hoots round the downspouts
And echoes from the drains.
There are howls
And chains clank.
There's a dungeon underneath our school
Where the caretaker takes care
Of everyone who's messed up on his floor
Or left chairs somewhere where a chair's no right to be.
I don't sleep easy any more—
Not since the handle of the PE cupboard door
Came right off in my hand.
Not since the incident with pancake batter
—It wasn't me, but nobody believes . . .
I don't sleep well.
At playtime I don't stray from the group.
He watches me.
I hold my breath when Miss sends us on messages.
Not me. Not me.
He'll get me one day,
On the corridor. Alone.
And then I'll go down one of those dark passages.

Jan Dean

The Horrible Horror . . .

It's a Horrible Horror from Outer Space
With question-marks instead of a face.

The air round me feels dripping and dank
Like a dustbin.
D'you hear that—plop—in the water-tank?
There's mildew on my skin.

Is it a robot? Is it a creature?
Why does it look like our Head Teacher?

There's something sniffing and snuffling its way
Along the lamp-posts in our street.
Its footsteps rattle like a tin tray,
Though it has no feet.

Is it a robot? Is it a creature?
Why does it look like our Head Teacher?

It's coming nearer and nearer and nearer
To our house. What I do?
Mrs Blunt says, 'Cucumbers are dearer
Today.' Mrs Hodge says, 'Spuds are too.'

Is it a robot? Is it a creature?
Why does it look like our Head Teacher?

It's at our gate. I'm going to scream.
It's huge, and hungry, and black.
I've woken up. It isn't a dream.
It is about to attack.

Is it a robot? Is it a creature?
Why does it look like our Head Teacher?

It's grabbed me. It lets out a roar.
It's chewing my socks and vest.
'Who are you?' I yell. It sneers, 'I'm your
Mathematics Test.'

Leo Aylen

AARRGGH!!!!!!!

Will it Be the Drill?

Boring thoughts in a dentist's waiting room

Nobody waiting here but me
and the goggly tropical fishes.
'Mr Pierce will be ready for you
in five minutes,' she said.
'He's just sharpening his drills.'
(Did she actually say that last bit?)
Same old pile of dusty magazines:
Country Life, Farmers' Weekly,
Drillers' Monthly . . . nobody ever reads them,
just flips the pages over nervously
all the time wondering, *Will it be the drill?*
Same old box of toys for little kids:
trucks, trains, teddies . . . bet there's
a power drill in there somewhere.
Same old tank of fluorescent fish . . .
supposed to calm you down.
Who are you staring at?
Mouth opening and closing . . .
I know what you're saying:
'Poor devil, you're for the drill.'
Wish I'd not told Mum
I didn't need her to come with me . . .
Glad I'm not a dentist:
peering and poking in gaping mouths,
prodding about in blackened ruins,
looking up grotty noses and into
hairy ears . . . bet they enjoy the drilling though:
ZZZZZZZZZZZZZZZZZZZZZZZZZZZZZZZZZZZZZZZZZZZ

whizzing and whining away there . . .
another helpless, strapped-down victim
successfully bored.
Same old posters on the wall . . .
I think she's coming . . . yes! Perhaps
there's been a power cut and his gadgets
won't work . . . perhaps he's gone home . . .
perhaps he wants to postpone me until 2020 . . .

'Come this way please.
Mr Pierce will drill you now.'

Eric Finney

The Grobblies

Up and down
And round and round
The Grobblies grobble
O'er the ground,
Waiting, waiting,
Set to spring
On some poor
Unsuspecting thing.
Be it child
Or dog or cat
The Grobblies grob it
Just like that.
Grobble grobble
Grobble grobble
You'll go all weak
Your legs will wobble,
Your skin will sweat
Your heart will pound
As groobs of Grobblies
Gather round.
Grobble grobble
Teeth and gums
You'll soon be grobbled
Down their tums.
So little one
Beware, beware,
The Grobblies are
Just lurking there
For little children
Just like you

Who think that Grobblies
Can't be true,
But, oh, they can
My little one,
Just one quick gobble—
THEN YOU'RE GONE!

Clive Webster

The Broomstick Train

Look out! Look out, boys! Clear the track!
The witches are here! They've all come back!
They hanged them high—No use! No use!
What cares a witch for the hangman's noose?
They buried them deep, but they wouldn't lie still,
For cats and witches are hard to kill;
They swore they shouldn't and wouldn't die—
Books said they did, but they lie! They lie!

Oliver Wendell Holmes

Why Does the School Seem So Scary?

Why does the school seem so scary?
Is it the fact that the Head
glows a faint green in the gloaming
and is most indisputably dead?

Or can it possibly be the pale teachers
who creep from their coffins at night
and prowl around, fangs sharp and gleaming,
searching for someone to bite?

Or the school secretary, that monster,
did she give the school a bad name
when she ate crossing lady, Miss Grommet,
and a plump school inspector called James?

Though perhaps it's the caretaker, Grubwort,
a demon from some nether hell
who stokes up the fires in the boiler,
a job which he does strangely well.

Maybe it's Kate, classroom helper,
with her warts and her tall witch's hat,
who sits muttering spells with the help of
an extremely peculiar black cat.

It can't be the pupils, or can it,
dragging their chains round the school,
all mouldering, gruesome, and ghastly;
perfectly cute little ghouls?

Is it the cook, who for dinner
serves eyeballs poached lightly on toast,
or the playground attendant, Miss Dreary,
that rather decrepit old ghost?

Could be the giant school bell, tolling,
the boom as the school doors are slammed,
the vultures who wheel round the turrets
or the agonized shrieks of the damned?

So, why does the school seem so scary?
It's a very good school, parents say
as they drop off their offspring at midnight,
safe from the grim light of day,

then shamble and lurch into shadow
with many a harsh, croaking call.
Some folk say, compared to the parents,
the school isn't scary at all!

Marian Swinger

Spider's Revenge

When you're running around in the garden
I think you should always take care.
Don't step on a spider, don't squash it,
Remember his father's out there.

His father could really be massive.
He'll hang about just out of sight.
He could use poison fangs to attack you.
If you stand on his child, he just might.

He'll lurk about deep in the bushes,
His hairy legs ready to pounce.
He could spin a thick web all around you
And leave you to starve, ounce by ounce.

So, if you are out in the garden,
I think you should always take care.
Don't step on a spider, don't squash it . . .
His father is out there, somewhere.

Ian Larmont

Earwig O!

They used to fear
That while asleep
Into the ear
This beast would creep;
Through waxy passages
Would tread
To penetrate
The very head,
Until at last
It would attain
The grey and wrinkled
Human brain
Where, after pausing
For the view,
It probably
Would start to chew . . .

Believe this,
You must be a dope.
It's just
An old wives' tale.

I hope.

Eric Finney

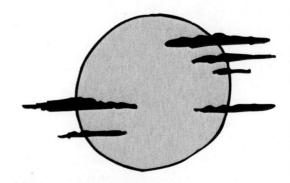

Lost in the Wild, Wild Wood

I'm lost in the wild, wild wood. I run,
wolves at my heels. I scream. The sun
has vanished into haunted gloom.
I hear scrabbling, panting, hear my doom.
Branches clutch, twigs tangle hair.
Brambles catch, my clothing tears,
to rags, to shreds. All tattered and forlorn
I stumble, gasping, like a wounded fawn
and the wolves, the great grey wolves, are
    circling round
as I sink fainting to the stony ground
upon the place I fell so long ago,
that place which no one living now can know,
where a small white bone or two still lies
and no one hears my thin and ghostly cries.
For the world I knew and loved has gone for good
and left me lost for ever in this wood.

Marian Swinger

Who?

Who is that child I see wandering, wandering
Down by the side of the quivering stream?
Why does he seem not to hear, though I call to him?
Where does he come from, and what is his name?

Why do I see him at sunrise and sunset
Taking, in old-fashioned clothes, the same track?
Why, when he walks, does he cast not a shadow
Though the sun rises and falls at his back?

Why does the dust lie so thick on the hedgerow
By the great field where a horse pulls the plough?
Why do I see only meadows, where houses
Stand in a line by the riverside now?

Why does he move like a wraith by the water,
Soft as the thistledown on the breeze blown?
When I draw near him so that I may hear him,
Why does he say that his name is my own?

Charles Causley

The House that Time Forgot

I went down the hill to the house today,
To the house that used to be home,
I stood at the gate and I had a good stare
And the doors and the windows were all still there . . .

Grey smoke rose from a chimney—
But how could there be a fire?
We left the fireplace all bricked up
And, I tell you, I am no liar!

Then, under a tree in the garden
Where apples would ripen and fall,
I saw the ghost of a girl in green
Bounce an invisible ball.

I heard a cry from a window
Where curtains waved in the breeze,
But we left the windows closed and locked—
I felt my body freeze.

Wait, I cried, to the ghostly girl,
As I started to open the gate
But the chimney stood smokeless, cold and still,
And the green girl would not wait.

So I tiptoed up to the window
Where I'd seen the curtains blow,
But I found them locked and shuttered—
As we'd left them years ago.

But under the tree, tall nettles and grass
Were trodden where someone had been:
I found the core of an apple
With teeth-marks in the skin.

The hairs on my neck were standing.
A shiver ran down my spine
When I saw a child in the shadows,
And the face of the child was mine.

I ran from the house that used to be home,
I raced to the top of the hill,
Then I woke in a stupor of sleep and delirium;
Somebody said I was ill.

My hair lay wet on my pillow,
A fever made my head hot,
But I clutched in my fist an apple-core
From the house that time forgot.

Celia Warren

Mossie

Don't ya mess wi me, pal,
my aim is true.
Stiletto in the shadows
hunting for you.

Nip ya on the finger,
armpit, neck, or knee;
Jag ya anywhur ah like,
ya can't stop me.

See them mobbing midgies,
gang a mugging fleas;
Na style, na class, just numbers,
there's none as brave as me.

Wasps are dumb and clumsy,
one stroke an they're dud,
they're just easily upset
but I'm out for your blood.

Sandflies are sneaky nippers—
I'm elegant and proud;
Hear me coming, human,
I'll be singing clear and loud.

I like to boast and dance around
before I get stuck in—
when you can't hear me then fear
cos I'll be sucking skin.

'Float like a butterfly,
Sting like a bee'—
man, I can do all that an' more,
you've no chance against me!

Dave Calder

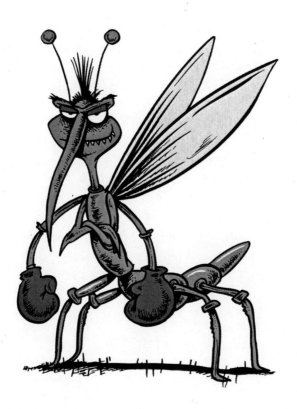

The Nishi's Call

Its call is the sound of hot molasses syrup,
of ripest mango and candyfloss tenderness.
It stalks the streets and passes below your window;
it stops outside your door and moans its wild distress.

It can sound like your loving mother, passed away,
or your dead father who once held you to his chest;
it can sound like your own sweet sister, brother,
    friend,
or your darling child, your nearest and your dearest.

Beware! The Nishi walks the night with piercing cry.
It's the most haunting creature you can imagine.
Don't answer the Nishi's call. It's a soul-snatcher
and your voice is a silver cord it will reel in.

The Nishi carries an empty earthen vessel
to trap your soul if you answer its tempting cry.
When morning comes, the Nishi's dead will rise again,
so close your mouth and ears or you will surely die.

A creature of night and of nightmares, the Nishi
stalks the streets and holds vigil below your window.
Its call is the sound of candyfloss tenderness.
Do not answer, for it will snatch your soul and go.

Debjani Chatterjee

NOTE: *The Nishi is part of Bengal's folklore. It is a creature of the night, who gathers the souls of the unwary, deceiving them by calling in a familiar voice.*

Who is It?

Go to the park
wHen it's dark.
whO do you see
swiSh silently
abouT the bushes?
who iS it pushes

Swinging swings,
uPending things,
knOcking gates,
thrOwing slates,
clanKing chains
acrosS the drains?

Who is it? Who?

Jill Townsend

Kidnapped!

Hey!
Let go.
What is this?
  It's got green hair
  and two pairs of ears.
  It's as big as a bear.
  It's pulled me out of my chair
    and now it's chasing me down the stairs.

Aaagh!
Help, someone!
It's grabbed me.
  It's got sharp teeth
  and these huge webbed feet.
  It's blue on top, purple underneath.
  I think it wants something to eat
    and it's dragging me out of our street.

Hello.
Anyone there?
I'm being kidnapped!
  It's got scaly toes,
  a belly button that glows,
  there's fire dripping from its nose.
  What? Fangs? It's got hundreds of those
    and it's hurrying me over these unlit roads.

Please—
get off!
Is nobody coming?
  It's got slippery skin,
  bulging eyes and luminous veins.
  Its fingers grip like freezing chains.
  Oh no, I think we're off again
    and it's rushing me along this winding lane.

Ah . . .
Oh dear.
Sorry about that.
  It's okay, I'm free,
  and I think that maybe
  I'd better say this very quietly
  because it was, after all, you see,
    just my own imagination running away with me.

David Horner

Don't Be Afraid

The ghosts that you see
In the dark of the night
Are no more, no less
Than a trick of the light.
And when you hear noises
That make your knees knock
It's wind in the trees
Or the chime of a clock.
The things that seem scary
Are all in your head
So don't be afraid
When you're tucked up in bed.

Then again, I could be wrong.
It might be the blood-dripping, child-eating monster
That lives under the floorboards outside your
   bedroom door.
Sleep tight!

Richard Caley

Acknowledgements

Every effort has been made to trace and contact copyright holders before publication and we are grateful to all those who have granted us permission. We apologize for any inadvertent errors and will be pleased to rectify these at the earliest opportunity.

Geraldine Aldridge: 'Toilet Monster' copyright © Geraldine Aldridge.
Leo Aylen: 'The Horrible Horror' copyright © Leo Aylen.
Matt Black: 'Just a Thought' copyright © Matt Black.
Martin Brown: 'Just the Usual Monsters' copyright © Martin Brown.
Dave Calder: 'Mossie' copyright © Dave Calder.
Richard Caley: 'Don't Be Afraid' copyright © Richard Caley.
Charles Causley: 'Who?' from *Collected Poems for Children,* published by Macmillan, used by permission of David Higham Associates.
Debjani Chatterjee: 'The Nishi's Call' copyright © Debjani Chatterjee.
Paul Cookson: 'Uncle John's Legs' copyright © Paul Cookson.
Sue Cowling: 'The Void' copyright © Sue Cowling.
Jan Dean: 'Taking Care' from *Wallpapering the Cat,* Macmillan 2003, copyright © Jan Dean. Used by permission of the author.
Richard Edwards: 'Our Pond' copyright © Richard Edwards.
Eric Finney: 'Don't Panic', 'Mr Alucard', 'Will it Be the Drill?' and 'Earwig O!' copyright © Eric Finney.
Bashabi Fraser: 'When the Moon Went Mad . . .' copyright © Bashabi Fraser.
Philip Gross: 'Trick of the Lights' copyright © Philip Gross.
Mark Halliday: 'The Cupboard Under the Sink' copyright © Mark Halliday.
David Horner: 'Kidnapped!' copyright © David Horner.
Mike Johnson: 'Nightmare Questionnaire' copyright © Mike Johnson.
Ian Larmont: 'Spider's Revenge' copyright © Ian Larmont.
Patricia Leighton: 'Someone at the Door' and 'The Fate of the Mary Belle' copyright © Patricia Leighton.
Kevin McCann: 'At Sunset' and 'Ghost-whispering' copyright © Kevin McCann.
Jeff Moss: 'A Night I Had Trouble Falling Asleep' from *The Butterfly Jar,* copyright © Jeff Moss.
Tim Pointon: 'Munch Menu' copyright © Tim Pointon.
Cynthia Rider: 'Whispers' copyright © Cynthia Rider.
Rachel Rooney: 'Making Friends' copyright © Rachel Rooney.